doodle on!

Christmas Doodles

Written by

Smriti Prasadam-Halls

Illustrated by

Anja Boretzki

Campbell Books

Written by
Smriti Prasadam-Halls

Illustrated by
Anja Boretzki

Campbell Books

First published 2009 by Campbell Books
an imprint of Macmillan Children's Books
a division of Macmillan Publishers Ltd
20 New Wharf Road, London N1 9RR
Basingstoke and Oxford
www.panmacmillan.com
Associated companies worldwide
ISBN 978-0-230-74421-9
Copyright © 2009 Macmillan Publishers Ltd
Printed in China
1 3 5 7 9 8 6 4 2

Christmas is coming! Write a letter to Santa Claus.

Decorate the Christmas tree! Put something special at the very top.

Hurray! It's started snowing! Fill the sky
with snowflakes.

Make this row of shops look festive.

Time to go Christmas shopping! Write a list of what you're buying and who it's for.

Add some amazing lights between these houses.

Design a dazzling display for this department store window.

What Christmas shopping have you bought?

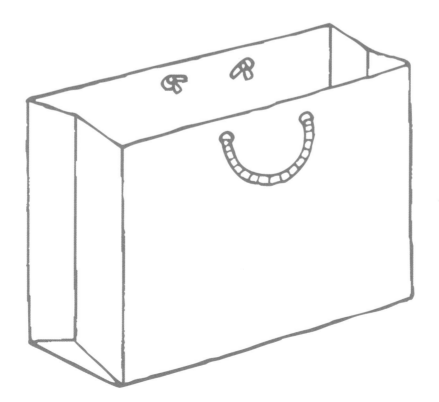

Decorate your Christmas wrapping paper.

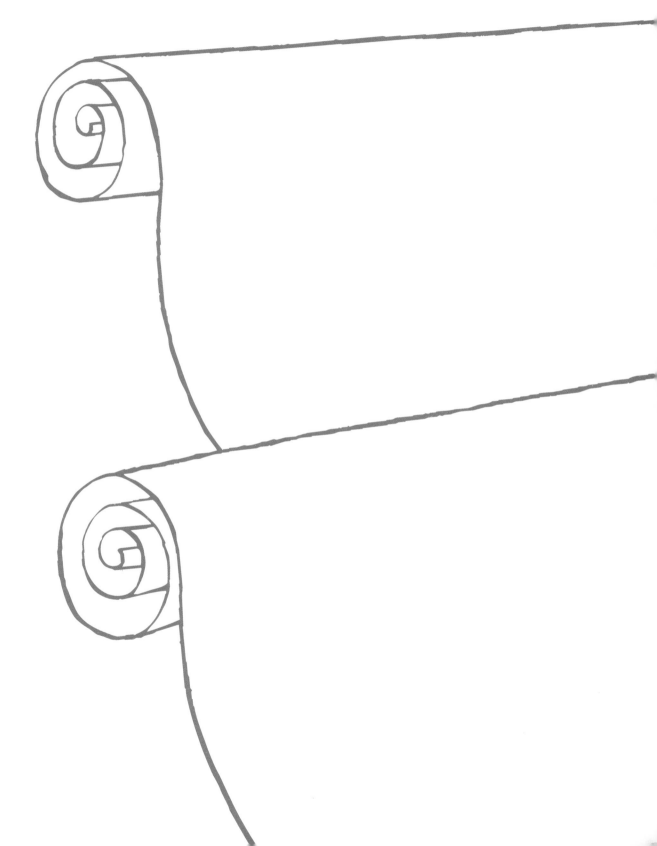

What's in Santa's big sack?

Complete the costumes for Santa's elves.

Decorate Santa's house in the North Pole.

Who's playing outside?

Design your own Christmas cards to send to
your friends.

Address these envelopes and give them special Christmas stamps.

Draw a postbox so you can post your cards.

It's a blizzard! Draw a snow plough clearing
the streets . . .

. . . and the snow banks it's made.

Who lives in this winter wonderland?

Add some more children and snowballs to this snowball fight!

Add some more sledges and the people on them!

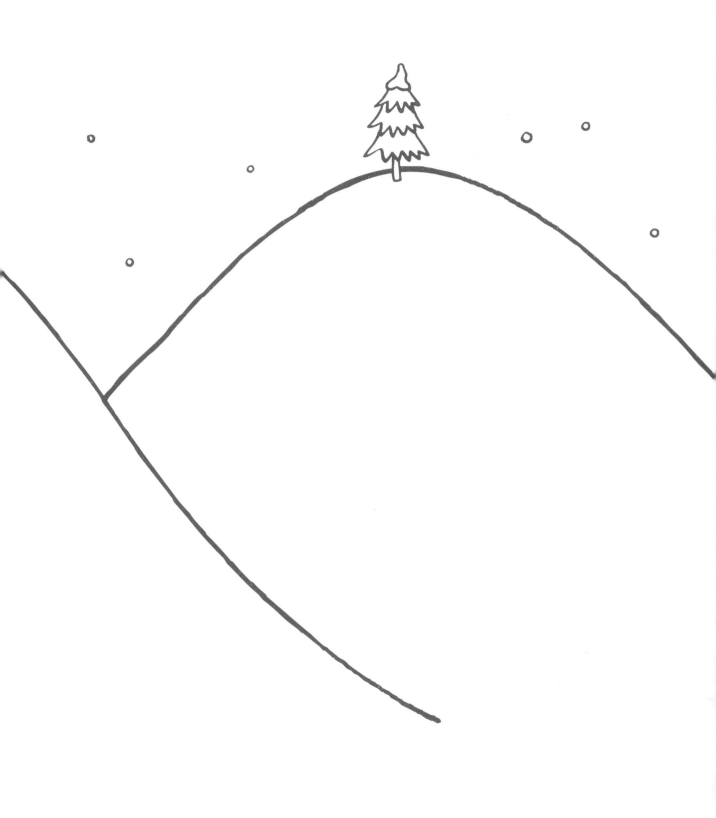

Finish off these snowmen.

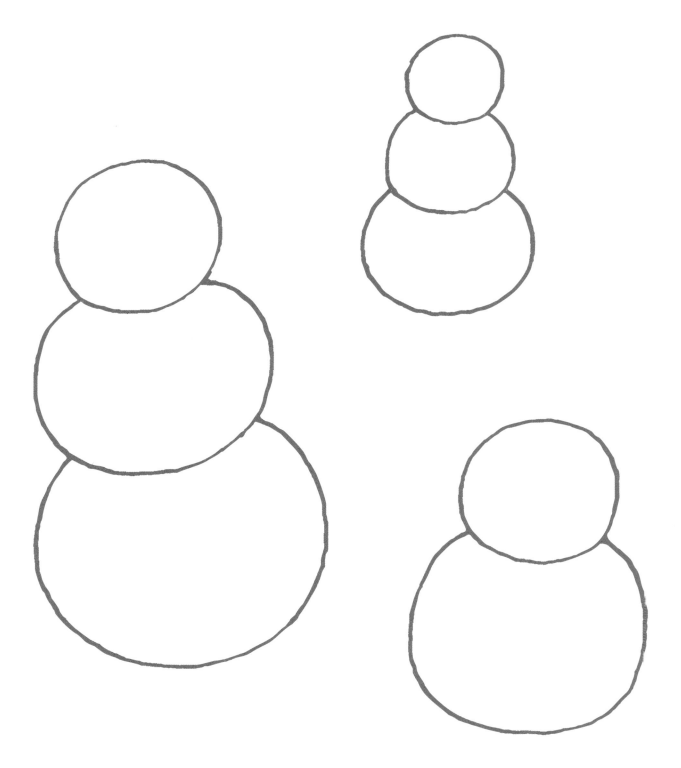

Get Santa ready for his big night.
Don't forget his hat and beard!

Invent a recipe for your own yummy Christmas treat.
Write the ingredients here.

Decorate these baubles for the tree.

Have a ride on Santa's Express Train!
Who's waving from the windows?

Add some Christmas decorations to this room.

Design some paper decorations of your own.

Who is kissing under the mistletoe?

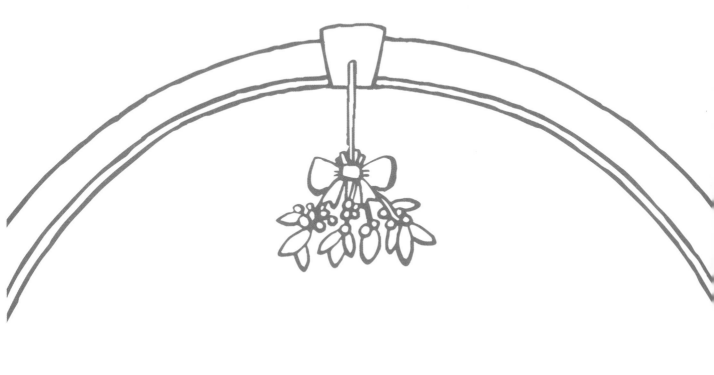

Santa's busy in his workshop.
What toys has he made?

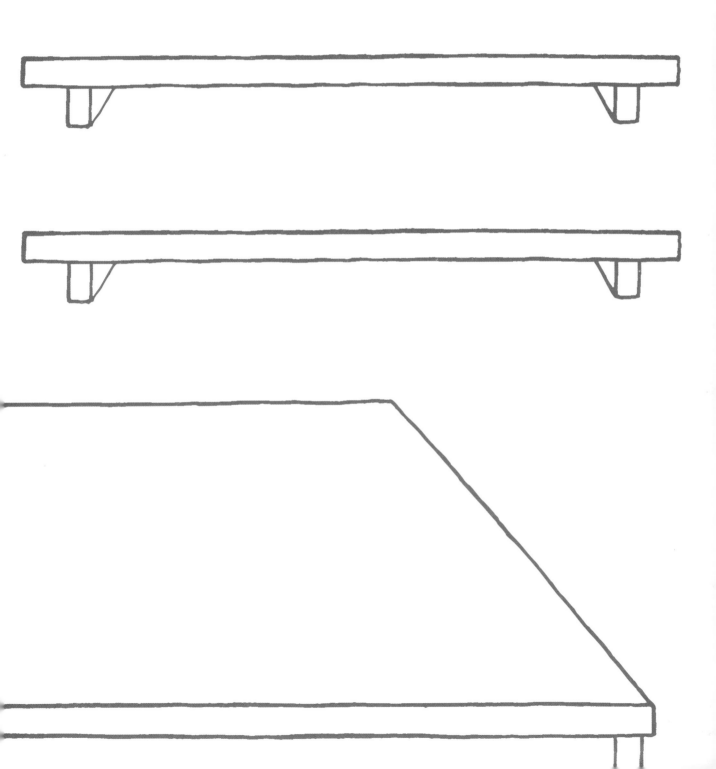

Decorate these mugs of hot chocolate
and add some tasty toppings.

What's outside your window on Christmas morning?

Decorate these houses with fantastic Christmas lights.

Design your own Advent calendar...

...what's behind the last door?

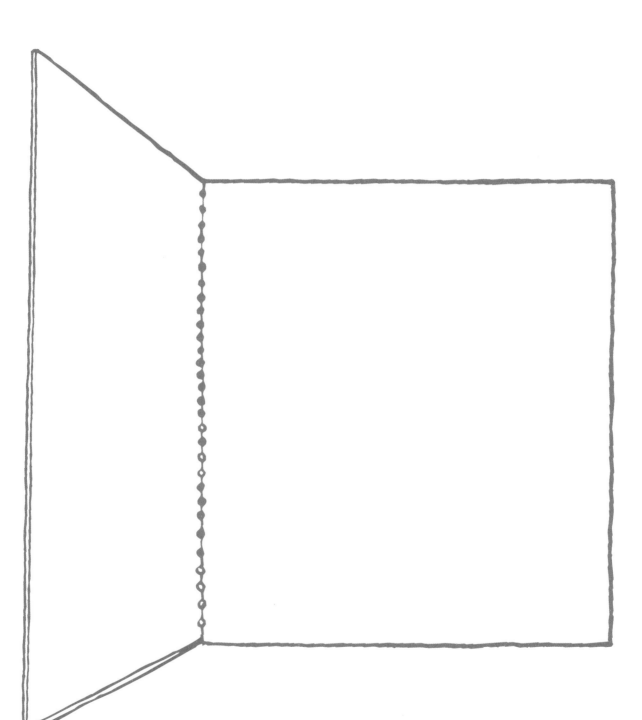

Wow! What is the postman delivering?

Decorate Mrs Claus' best Christmas outfit.

Design the silliest woolly hat!

And decorate the silliest mittens!

Decorate Santa's sleigh and add his reindeer.

Hang a wreath on these doors.

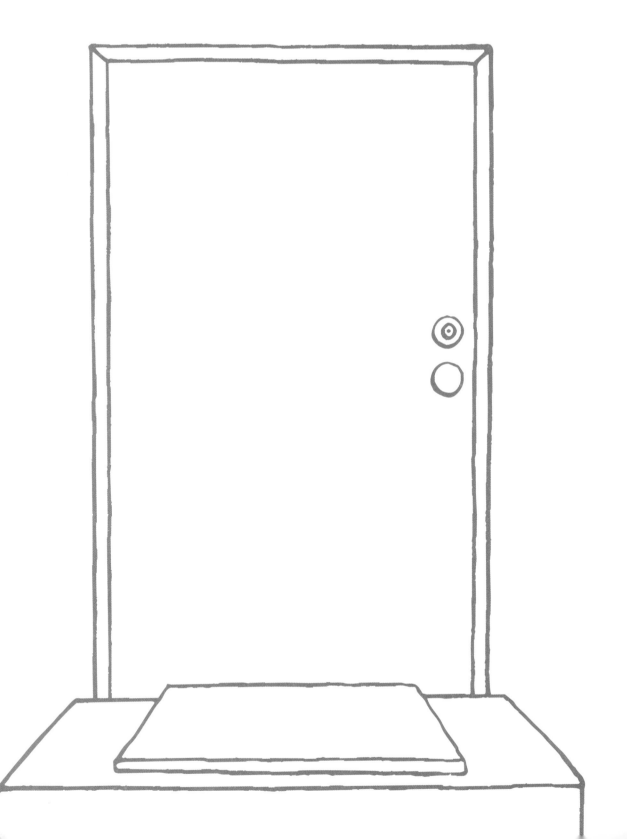

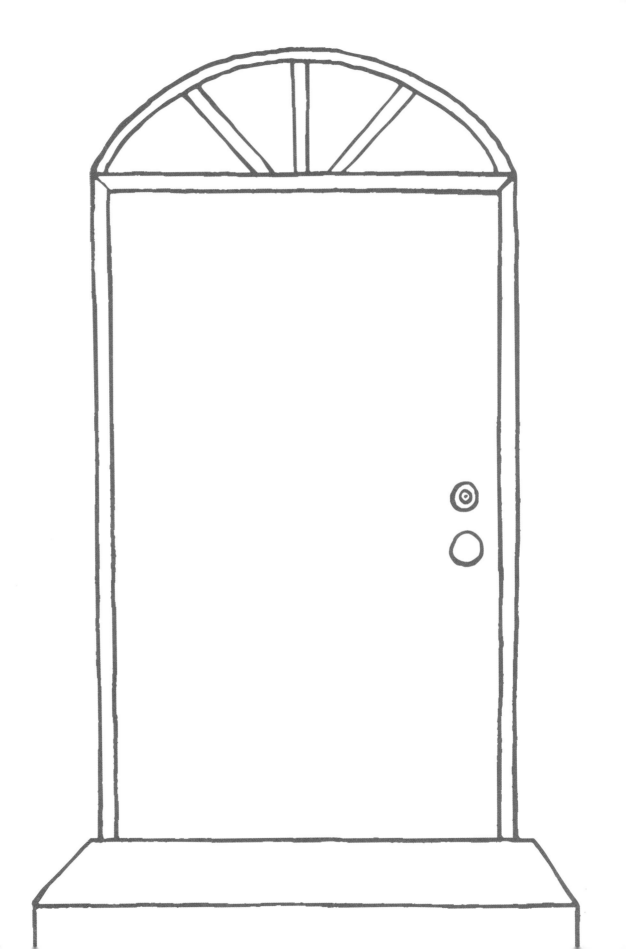

Line the mantelpiece with Christmas cards
and decorations.

Brrrr . . . it's freezing cold. Cover this house with icicles.

Add some logs and flames to this festive fireplace.

These animals have had lots of fun in the snow.
Draw in the prints that each one has left behind.

Draw some birds snuggling up on these branches.

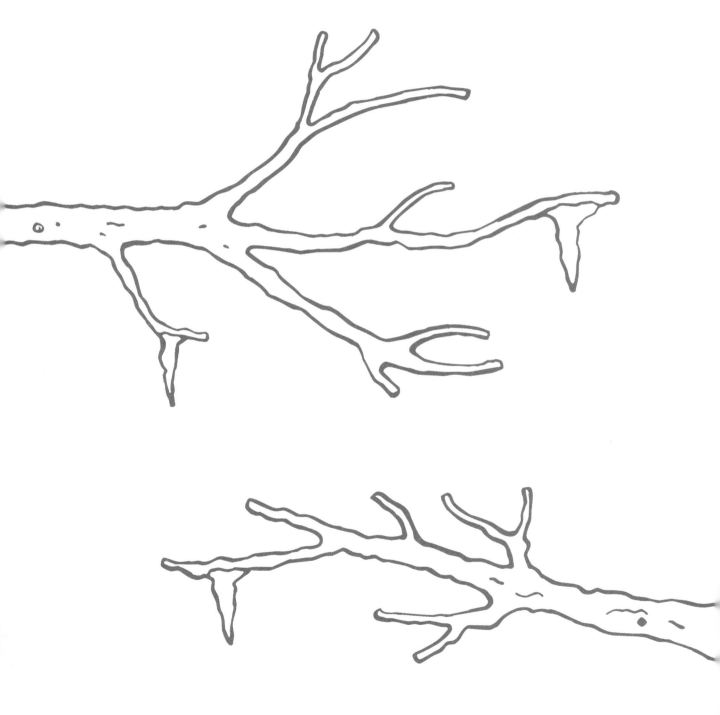

Ding dong! Who has come to pay you a
Christmas visit?

Draw some of the people in your family . . . and the gift they'd most like to receive!

Draw the biggest holly bush ever!

Decorate these candy canes!

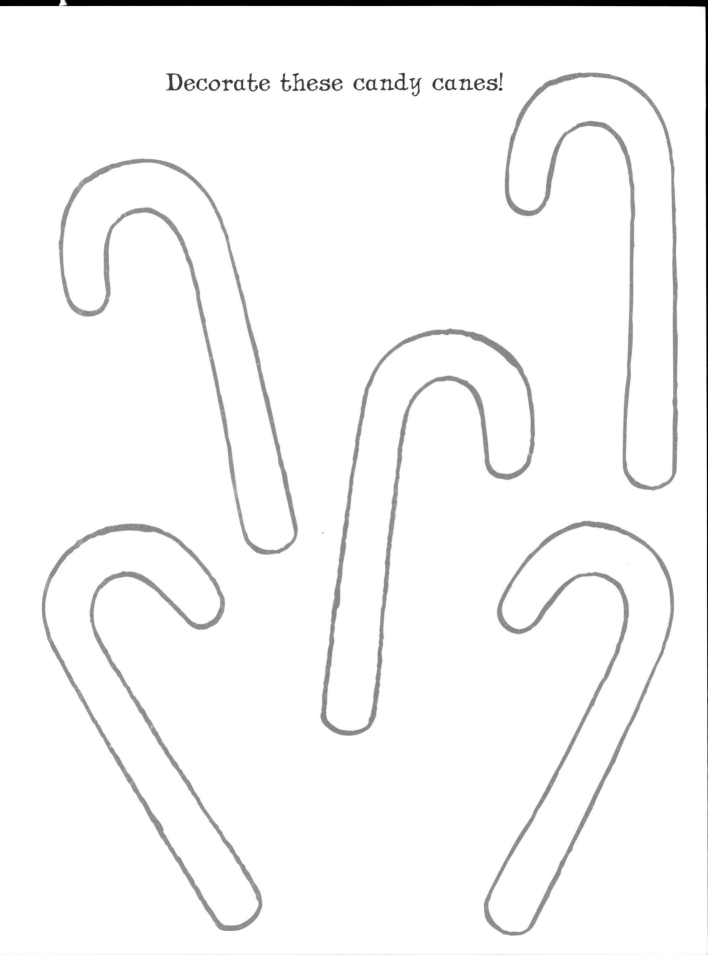

Wrap everyone up in warm winter woollies.

Look at the amazing snow fort they've made!

Can you dress these dogs in some winter outfits
to match their owners?

Decorate these Christmas gifts with patterns, bows and ribbons!

Decorate his Christmas apron . . .

... and then decorate the Christmas cake.

Who's at the Christmas party?

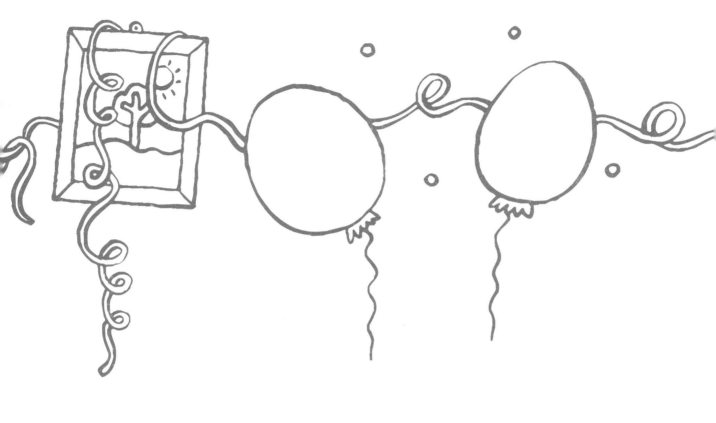

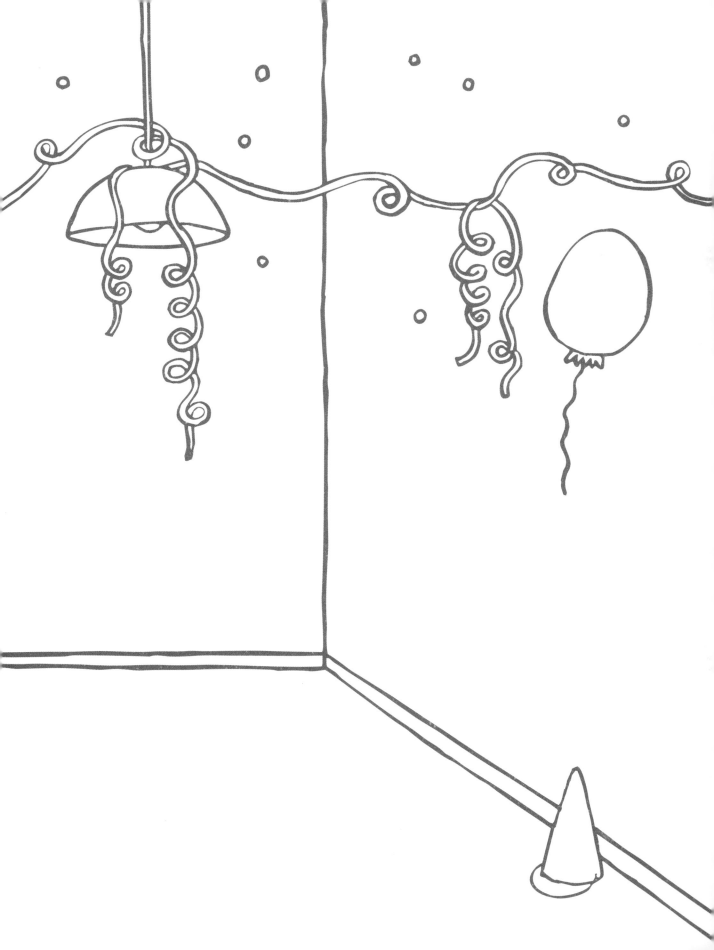

Draw lots more jingle bells.

Fill his trolley with Christmas shopping.

What are these pets getting for Christmas lunch?

Give antlers to the reindeer.

Hang some stockings under the mantelpiece.

Fill Santa's sleigh with gifts.

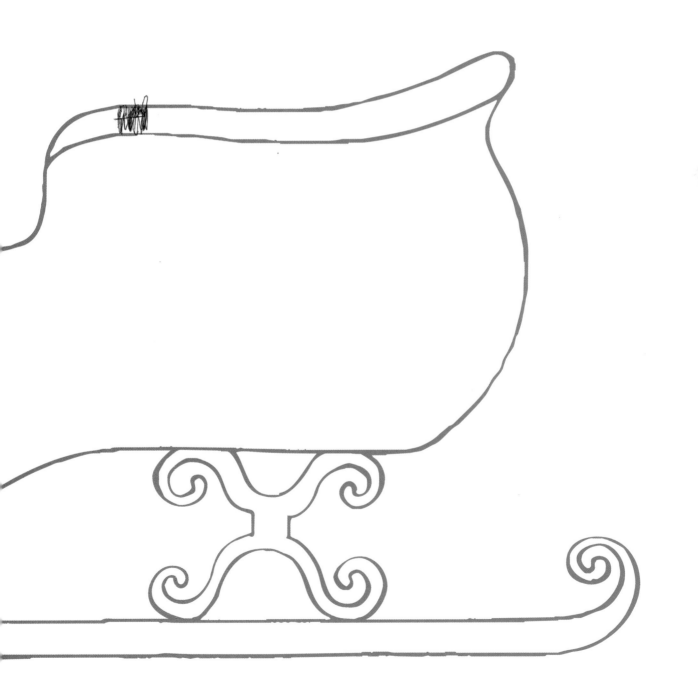

Put out a tray of treats for Santa . . .

... and something for the reindeer too.

Make a list of Christmas hopes and wishes.
Let's see if they come true!

Tuck everyone up in bed. Shhhhh!

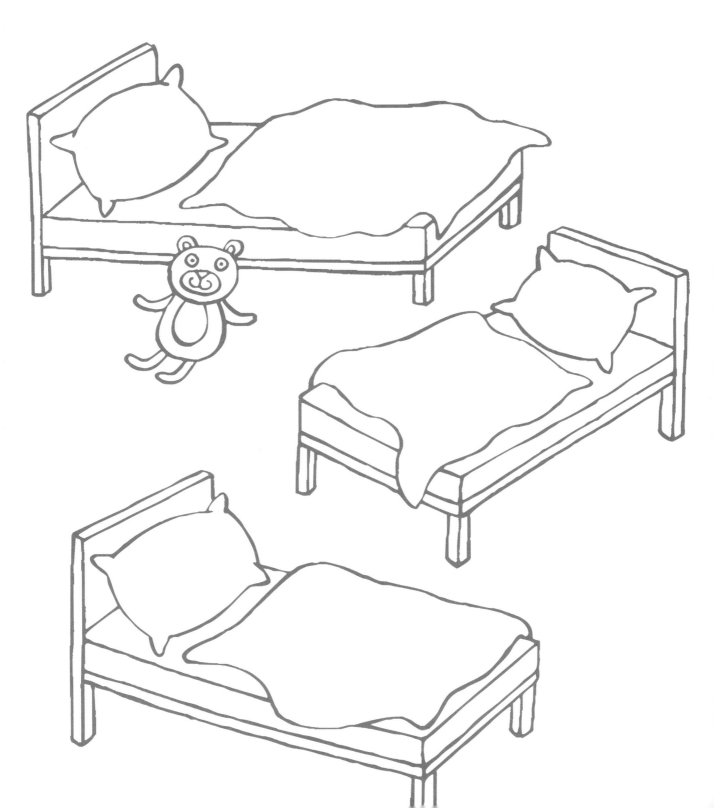

Bake a tray of Christmas cookies and decorate them.

Who has come to visit for the holidays?

Uh-oh! Santa is stuck in the chimney!

It's Christmas Eve! What are you dreaming about?

Design her favourite festive pyjamas.

What's for breakfast?

Don't forget to fill in the gift tags on your presents.

What presents did you get in your stocking?

Hee hee! Decorate Dad's Christmas jumper.

Give Mum some festive earrings.

Build the best snowman EVER.

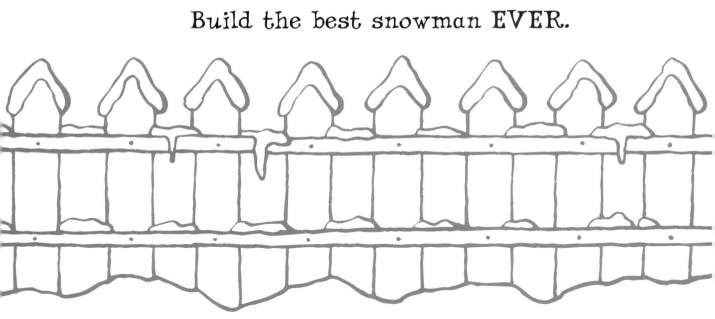

Decorate these mince pies.

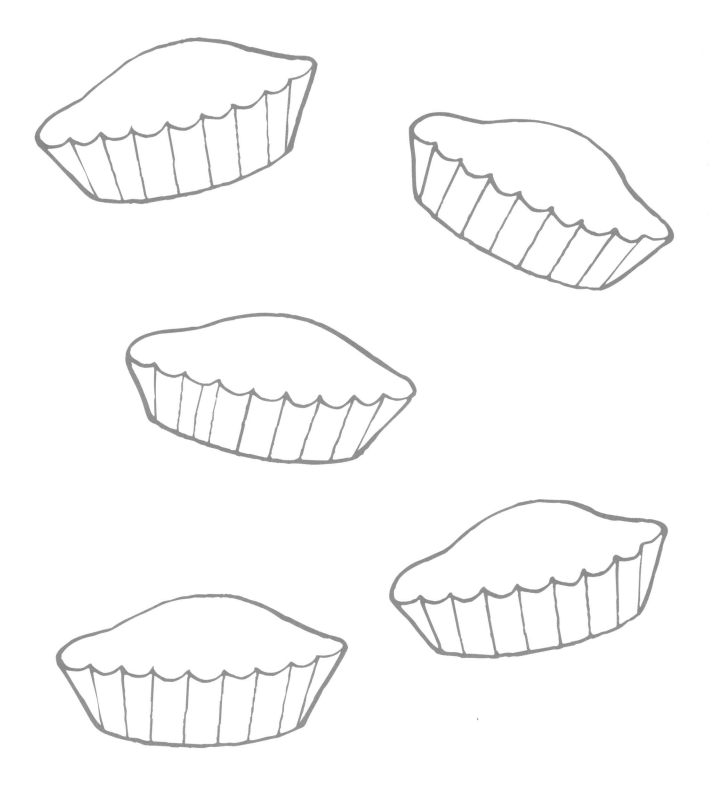

Help set the table for Christmas lunch!

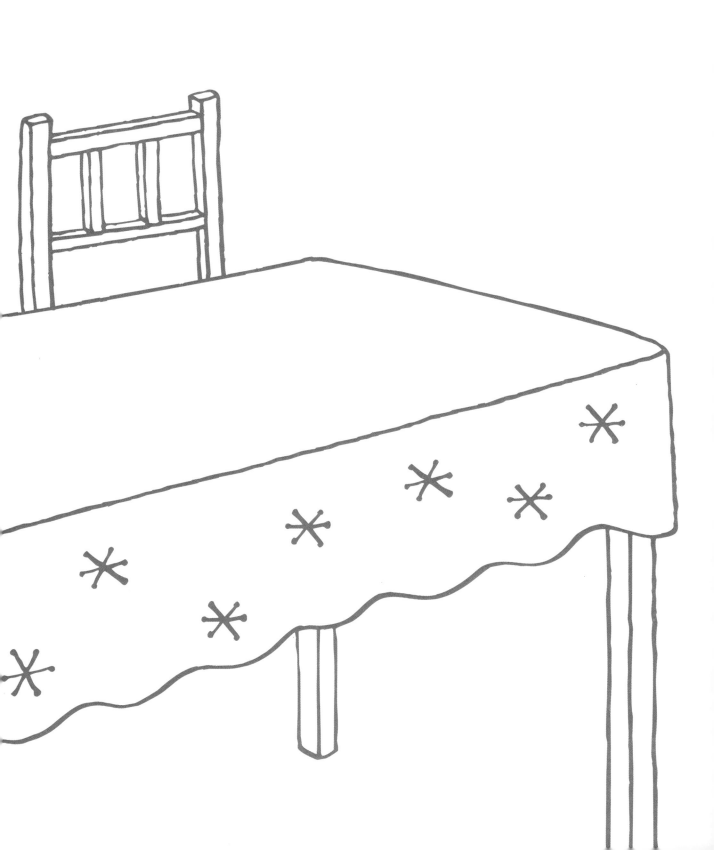

Now help put out all the food!

Give everyone party hats.

Decorate the Yuletide log.

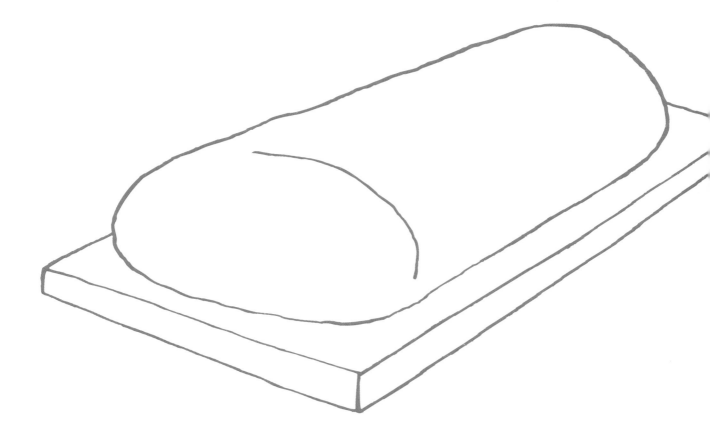

Who's singing carols?

Pull some crackers! What gifts came out?

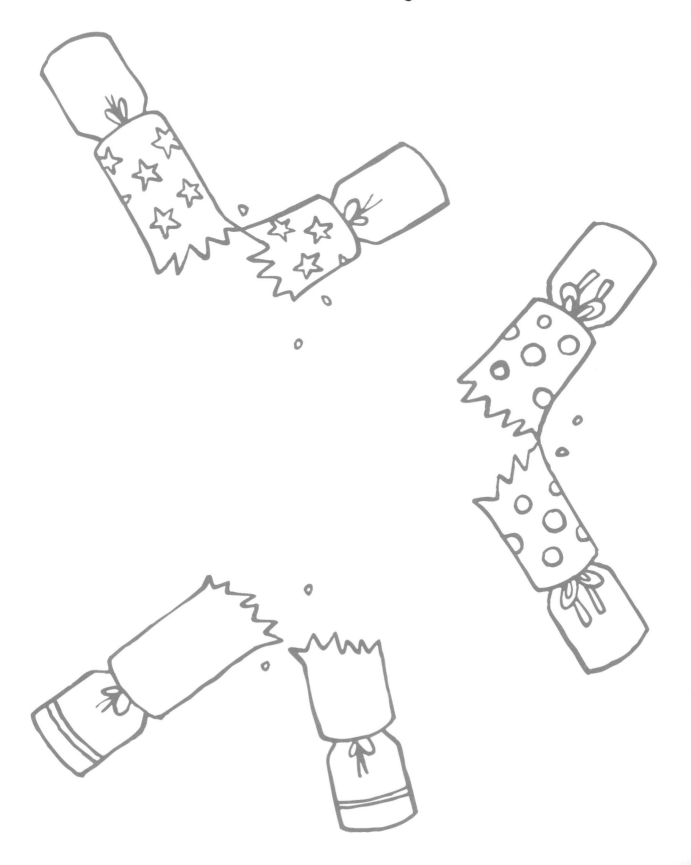

Draw your best present here.

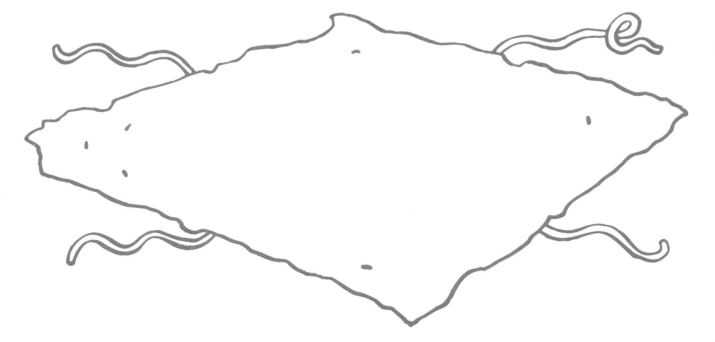

What's your favourite thing to eat at Christmas?

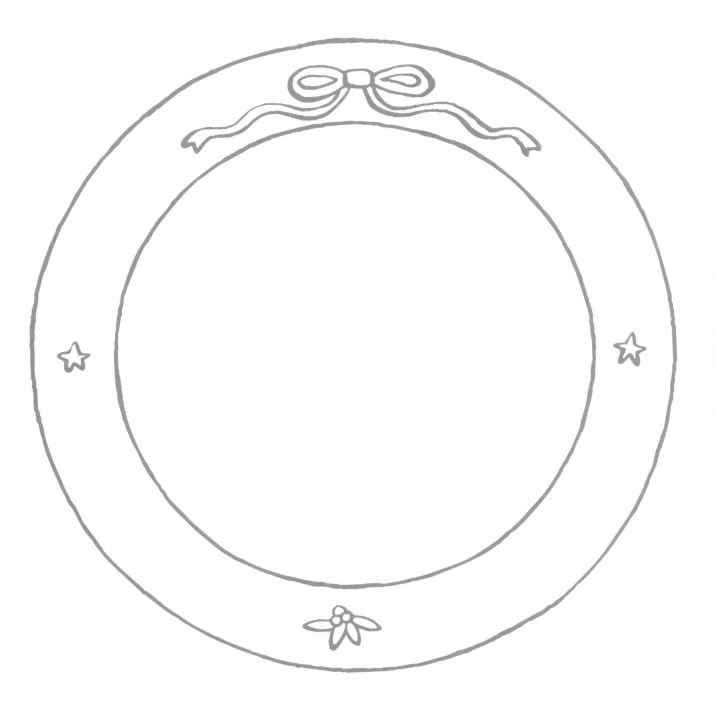

Design a fun game to play.

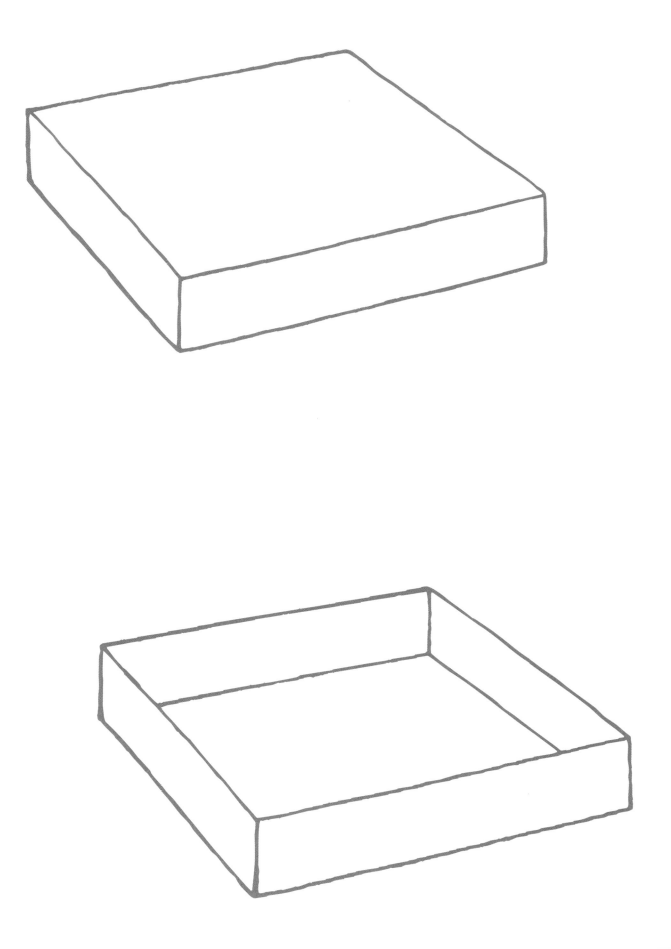

Click! Draw everyone in this Christmas family photo.

Draw some very silly photos from the day.

Design the cover of this book of Christmas stories.

Who is snoozing on the sofa?

Add some delicious chocolates to this box.

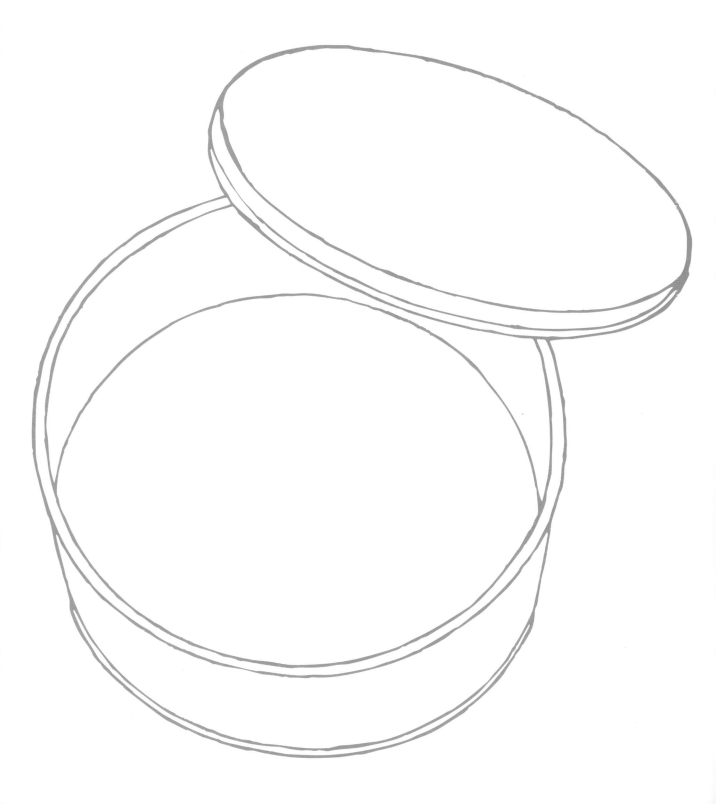

Hang some lanterns on the trees outside.

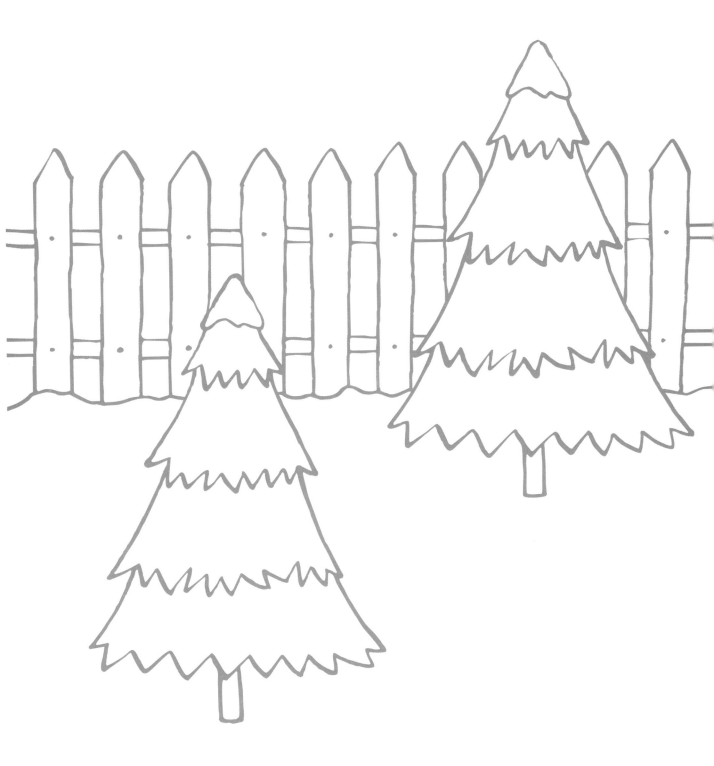

Who is singing round the piano?

Decorate this sledge!

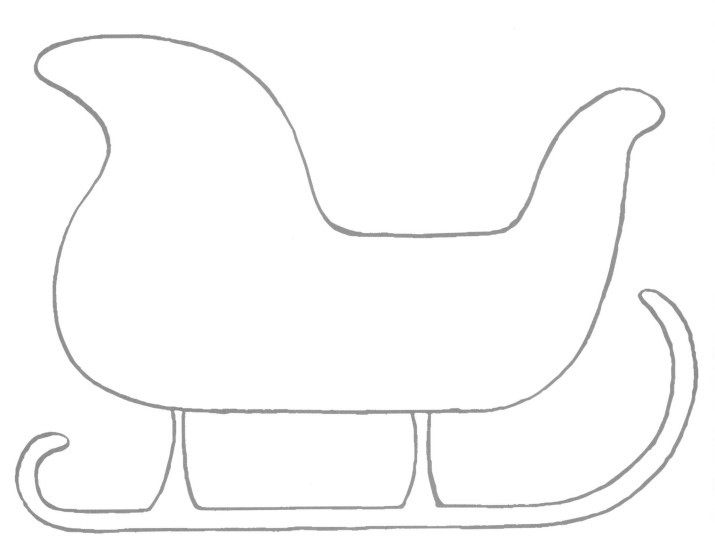

Decorate the park with fairy lights.

Time to go ice skating. Add some more skaters to the rink.

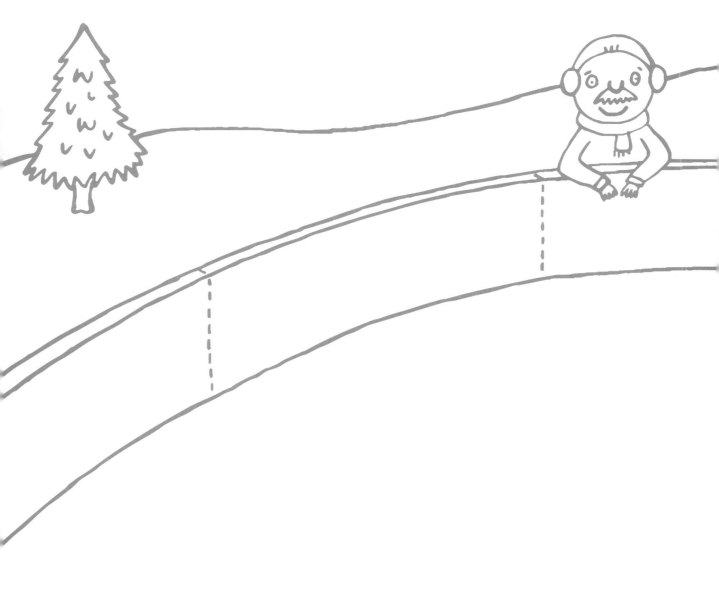

Create a giant Christmas tree for this town.

Draw the poster for the Christmas pantomime.

Who's on stage at the Christmas pantomime?

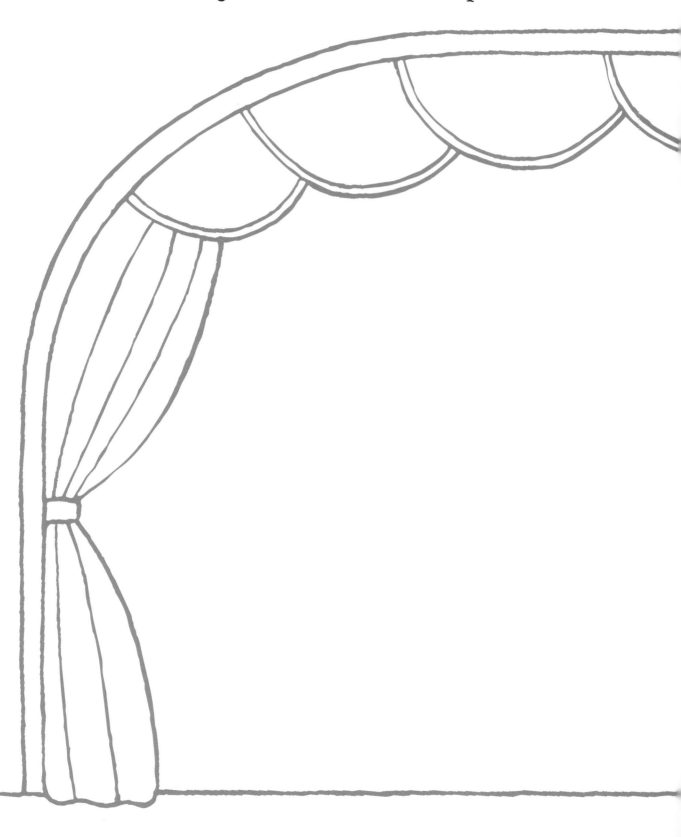

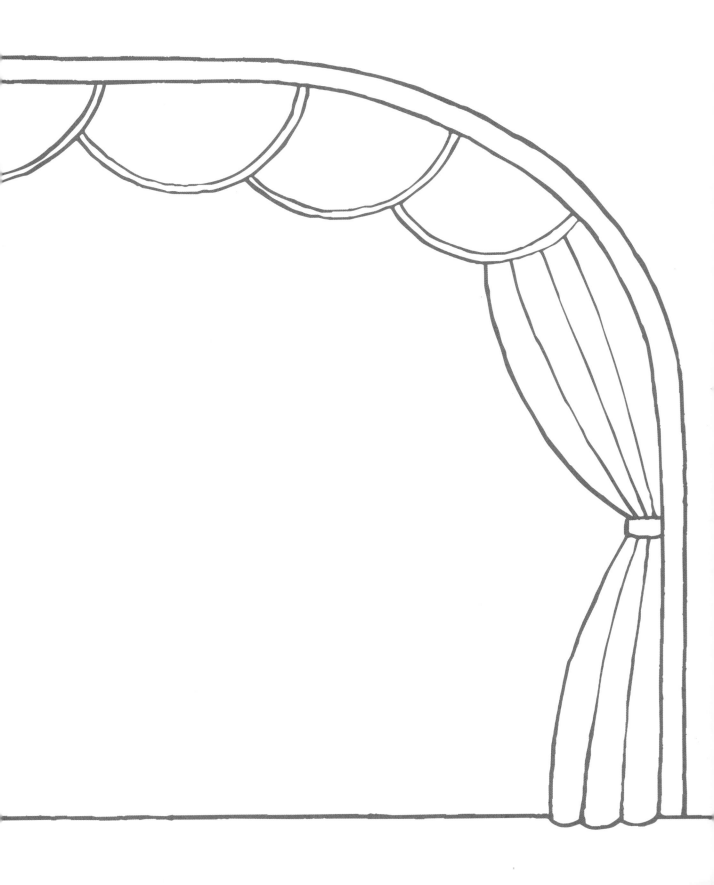

What can you buy at this Christmas market?

Give these busy shoppers lots of shopping bags.

Create a fantastic gingerbread house.

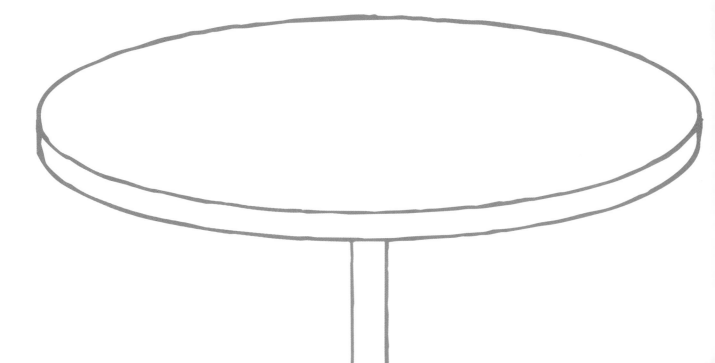

Decorate the delicious gingerbread men.

Copy a famous poem or carol – or make up one of your own.

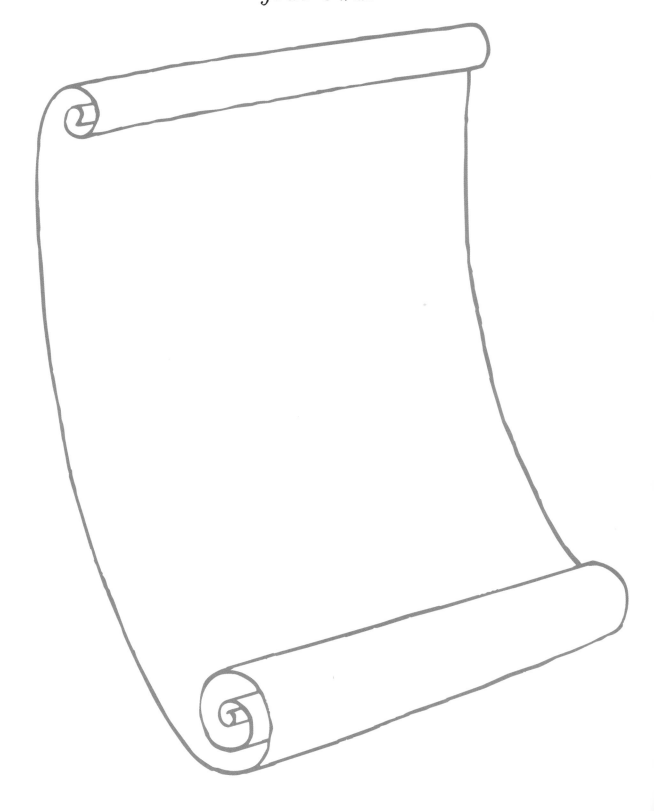

Write some Christmas cracker jokes here –
which one is the funniest?

Watch your favourite movie on TV.

Dad's having a snooze – have some fun and decorate HIM!

Add some more cars stuck in the snow.

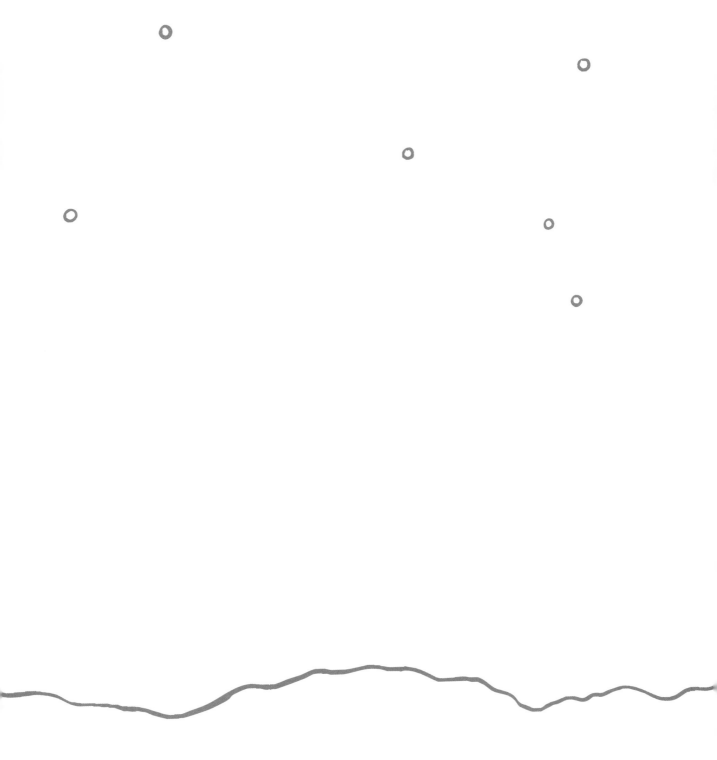

Take your new bike out for a spin.

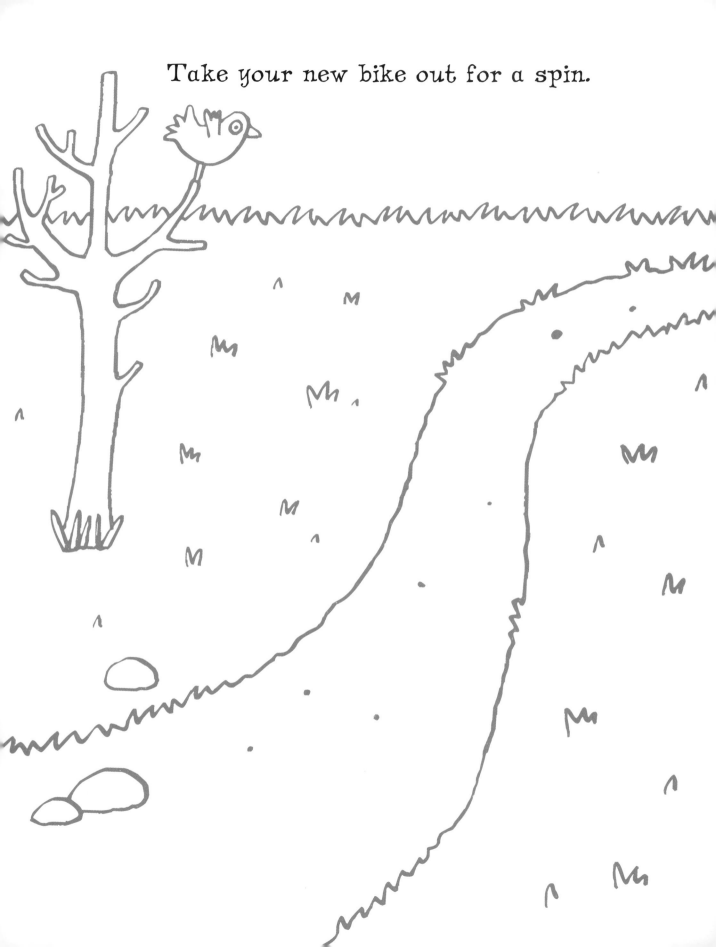

What new computer game are you playing?

Make a strange sandwich using leftovers from the fridge!

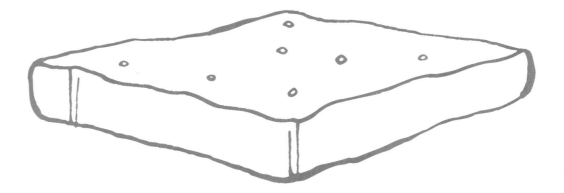

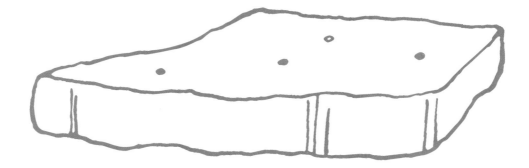

Get crafty with your old Christmas cards.

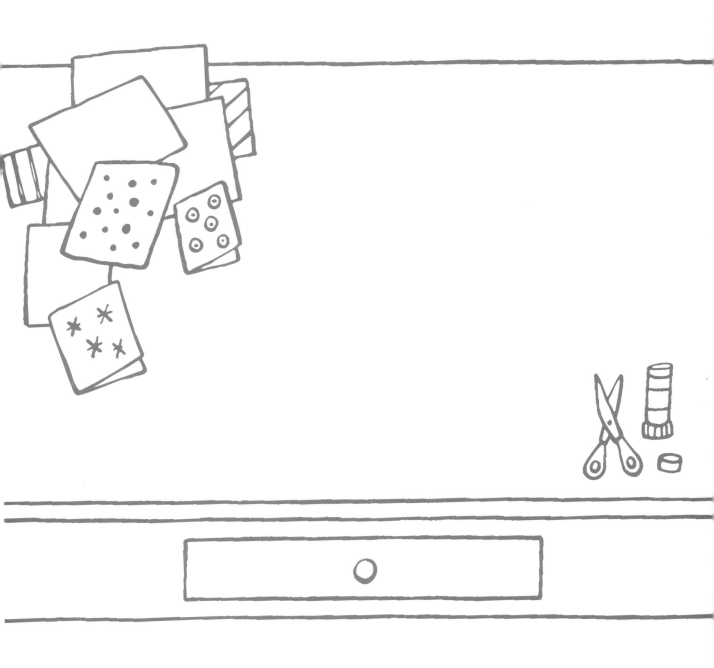

Draw pictures of the people you had fun with this christmas. Write their names too.

Write some thank you letters and decorate the notepaper.

It's New Year's Eve! Get the house ready for a party.

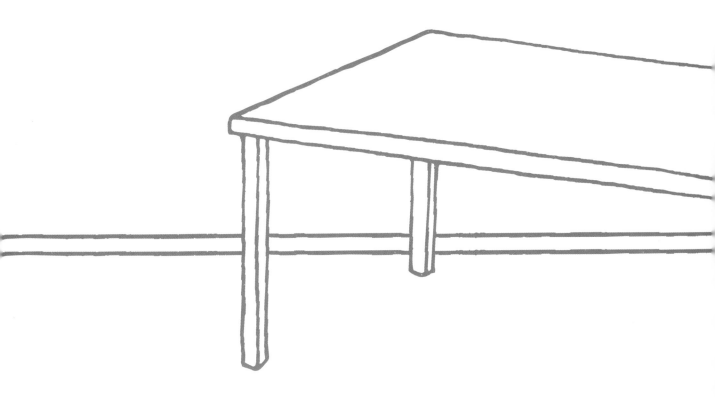

What are we going to eat? Fill the bowls
with snacks.

Write some questions for a quiz.

· NEW YEAR QUIZ ·

Who has fallen asleep trying to wait up for the new year?

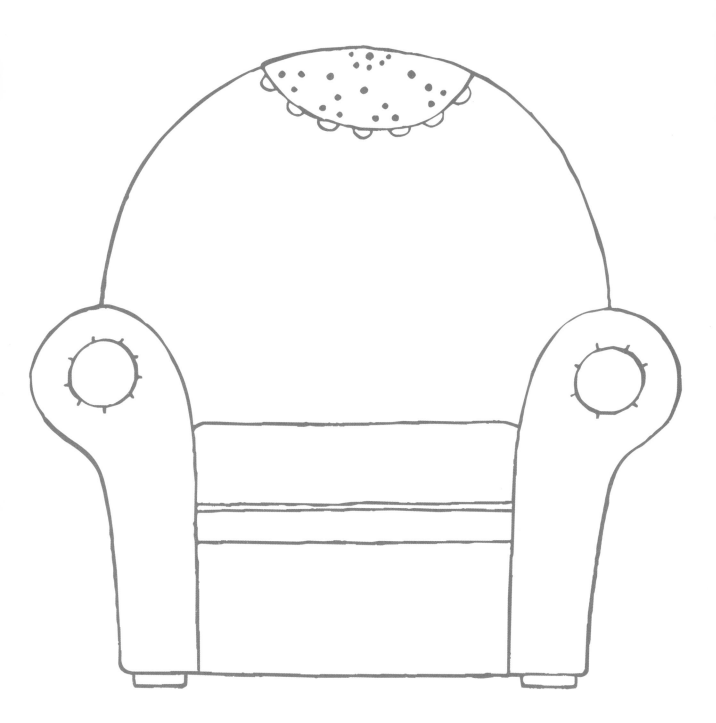

Set the hands of the clock to midnight.

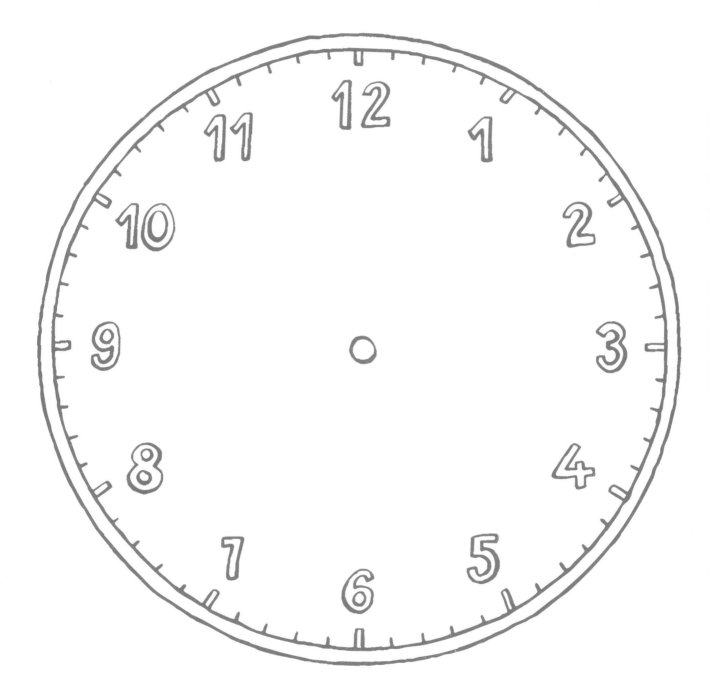

Wheee! Let off all the party poppers!

Make a list of your New Year's Resolutions.

Fill the sky with spectacular fireworks.
Happy New Year!